To: London

Wishing You All
the Best

Kimberly Rowland

# Nora's Lollipop

By Dr. Kimberly Rowland

Illustrations by Jamil Burton

## Dedication

To the inspiration behind this story, my daughter Taylor.  May your life possess knowledge of the past, understanding of your present, and wisdom for your future.  Above all, continue to honor your right to become your true, authentic self, as you were created to be.

To my mother, Alberta Edwards,
for her continuous love and support throughout my life.

To my cousin/brother, Dr. Kenneth R. Hamilton, Sr.,
for your continued support, encouragement and wisdom.

## Acknowledgements

Finally, to those individuals who supported my first children's book:
My sister Keisha Hill, Dr. Starlene Simons,
Wanda Ali, Jerry Glover, ,
Troy Balkum, Diana Bradshaw,
Terrie Carter, Antonio Sabas, Cheryl Washington, Kitisha Bush,
Maria Hamilton and Rick McCormack

May the seeds you have sown into this project be multiplied a thousand-fold.

Nora lay sleeping in her bed when her mother walked in to wake her up for school.

"Good Morning, sweetheart. Guess what today is?" asked Nora's mother.

"It's my birthday Mommy!
Did you make the cupcakes for my party?" asked Nora.

"Yes, sweetie, I did. Now let's get moving. This is a big day for you!"

Nora quickly moved to the bathroom and began to get dressed.

As she walked out the door, Nora kissed her Dad, dog
and brother, then skipped towards the car.

She threw her book bag in the back seat
and waited patiently to be driven to school.

When she got to school, Nora stepped out of the car and smiled at her teacher.

"Good morning, Nora," said Mr. Hamilton.  With a large grin, Nora exclaimed,
"Good Morning, Mr. Hamilton.  Today is my birthday!"

"I know Nora.  Happy Birthday to you!  We have a special
surprise for you today," said Mr. Hamilton.

"I know what it is already.  I am going to receive a big lollipop, like all the
other children did when it was their birthday!" Nora answered back.

"That is correct.  We will also have time for milk and cupcakes," replied Mr. Hamilton.

"Yippee!" Nora responded happily.

"Okay, class, let's all go inside," directed Mr. Hamilton.

"Everyone, today is Nora's birthday. Let's all sing Happy Birthday together, on the count of three," said Mr. Hamilton.

"One, two, three,"
"HAPPY BIRTHDAY TO YOU,

HAPPY BIRTHDAY TO YOU,

HAPPY BIRTHDAY, DEAR NORA,

HAPPY BIRTHDAY TO YOOOOUUUU!" everyone sang.

"Nora, now we have a big surprise for you! Here is your lollipop!!" exclaimed Mr. Hamilton.

"Since we are having cupcakes later, I am going to ask that you put your lollipop away and take it home for later, okay?" asked the teacher.

"Okay Mr. Hamilton" Nora answered.

Nora turned to the class and thanked everyone.

"Thank you all for my lollipop and singing Happy Birthday to me," Nora happily said to her classmates.

Mr. Hamilton said, "Nora, please pass out your cupcakes to all of the
students." Nora walked around swiftly, handing out cupcakes to her classmates.

She reached Walker's desk and delivered his cupcake. "Thank you, Nora.
How old are you today?" Walker asked. "I am the same age as you are Walker.
I am seven today," Nora responded, while smiling at him.

"I am eight, so you are not the same age as me," Walker replied with an attitude.
"You make me sick, Walker. You think you know everything," Nora snapped back
as she rolled her eyes. Nora continued to hand out cupcakes.

"Thank you for my cupcake, Nora, and happy birthday!" replied Taylor. "Thank you,
Taylor," Nora answered. "Would you like another cupcake? Maybe I will let you have Walker's cupcake,"
Nora teased, sticking her tongue out at Walker.

"I'll tell Mr. Hamilton on you if you do," Walker said.

"No thank you, Nora," Taylor replied. Then while looking at Walker and whispering in Nora's ear,
Taylor said, "We'll just ignore him during recess!" "Yeah, so you better be nice," Nora yelled at Walker.

"Humph, Brian and I will make you eat mud pies and get your clothes dirty," Walker replied.

"Is everything ok, Nora? Did you finish handing out your cupcakes?" Mr. Hamilton asked.
"Walker said he was going to get my clothes dirty during recess," Nora replied.

"Walker, is that true?" Mr. Hamilton asked.
"I was just teasing her, Mr. Hamilton," Walker replied.

Mr. Hamilton addressed Walker. "You are not to be disrespectful in our class.
Now, please apologize to Nora and behave yourself!"

A few moments went by and it was time for recess! "Okay, everyone, let's go outside for recess. You all have 30 minutes to play. Enjoy!" said Mr. Hamilton.

All the children walked outside for recess. Everyone was talking and surrounded Nora.

"Nora, what do you think you are going to get for your birthday?" Adam asks. "I already got the best present in the world, and it's my lollipop," Nora responded. "It's just candy on a stick! Last month I got a wagon and a fire truck for my birthday," Walker bragged.

"For my birthday, my parents took me to Disney," replied PJ. "My Mommy gave me a bracelet," Taylor added. "I had the biggest party ever!" Adam exclaimed. "Someone told me that only 10 kids showed up to your party," Walker said to Adam with a smirk, making everyone laugh.

"All of my best friends
showed up, and that's why you were not invited, Walker," Adam yelled.

"All I wanted was a lollipop, and I can't wait to take it home!" exclaimed Nora.

Mr. Hamilton stood outside and began to gather the children together. "Everyone, recess is over. It's time to go back inside," he said.

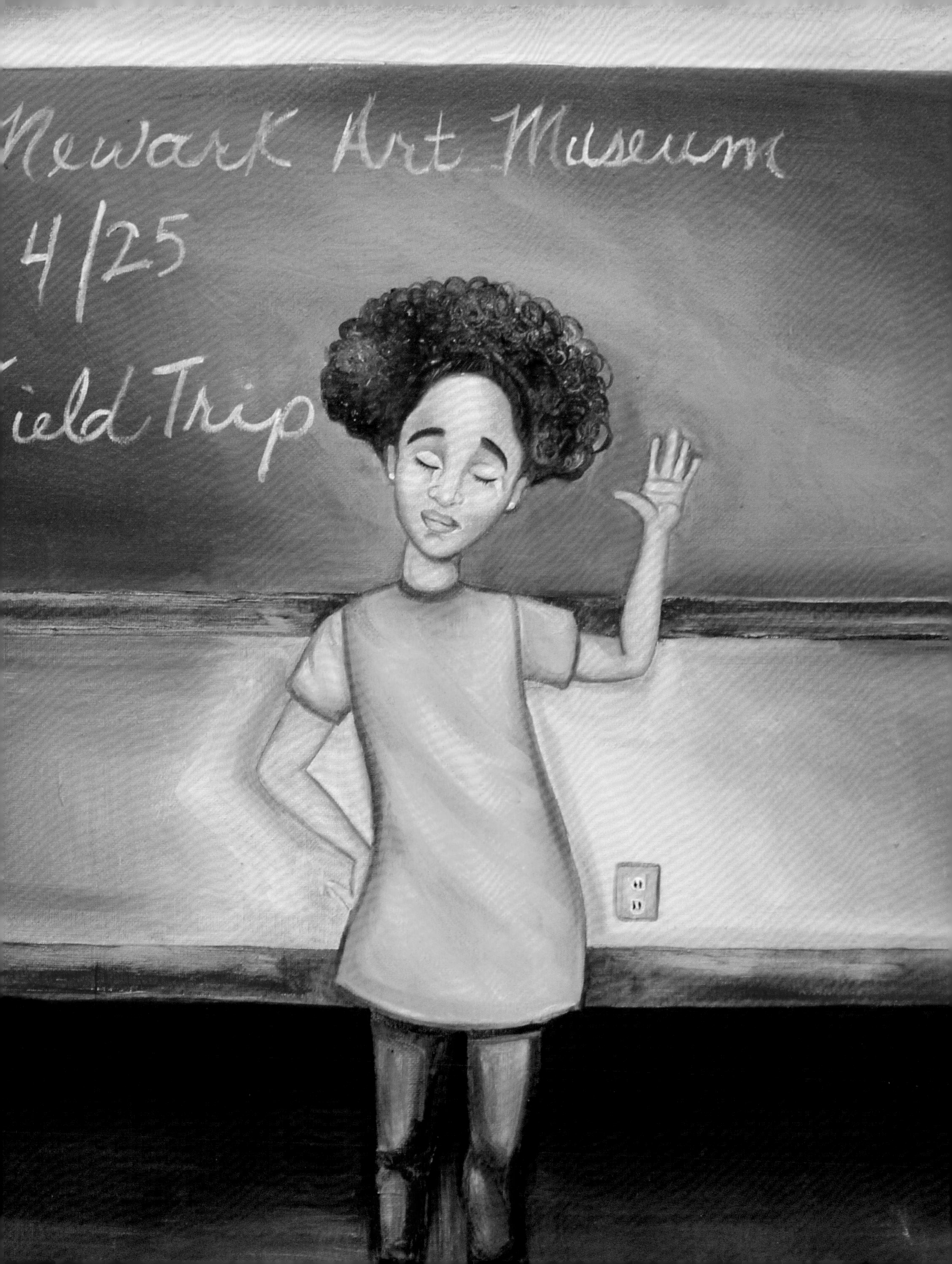
Newark Art Museum
4/25
Field Trip

"Where is it?" Nora screamed and began to cry.

Seeing her upset, Mr. Hamilton asked, "Where is what, Nora?"

"My lollipop! It's gone. Who took it? Someone took it!" Nora screamed.

"Please calm down, Nora. It has to be somewhere and we will find it. Has anyone seen Nora's lollipop?
If so, please bring it to the front of the room," Mr. Hamilton said.

"Who would take a stupid lollipop?" Walker asked.

"Okay everyone, enough!!! If someone does not tell the truth about Nora's lollipop, you will all be punished and there will be no recess for any of you tomorrow!" Mr. Hamilton exclaimed impatiently.

Adam suddenly stood up. "Oh alright, I confess. I ate the lollipop!" Adam said.

Everyone looked at Adam. "You did?" asked Mr. Hamilton.

"Nooooooooooooo, but I want to go to recess tomorrow," Adam shouted.

"Adam, you should never take the blame for something you did not do. Now have a seat," whispered Mr. Hamilton.

"Wake up, PJ! We are all searching for Nora's lollipop and you have to help too," said Taylor.
PJ got up and his lips were blue, red, and green.

Mr. Hamilton looked at him and said, "PJ, did you eat Nora's lollipop?"
Nora watched with tears running down her face.

"It was soooo good! Nora, I am very sorry. I just couldn't resist,"
answered PJ, as he too began to cry.

"PJ, what you did was very naughty and I believe that you owe
Nora a big apology," said Mr. Hamilton.

"I am really sorry, Nora, for eating your lollipop," PJ replied
as he wiped tears from his face.

Nora wiped her face and looked at PJ,
thinking about his apology.

"I forgive you, PJ. It was just a lollipop," Nora said kindly, while giving PJ a hug.

"Thank you Nora for having such a forgiving heart!" Mr. Hamilton said. He opened his desk drawer and gave Nora an even bigger lollipop.

Nora smiled happily because she got her lollipop after all!

## ABOUT THE AUTHOR

Kimberly Nicole Rowland is behind this beautiful and touching narrative that affirms love is understanding, kind and forgiving.

Kimberly Nicole Rowland graduated from Seton Hall University with a Master's of Arts degree in Strategic Communication & Leadership. She also earned her doctorate degree from University of Maryland University College in Management Organizational leadership & Technology.

Kimberly Nicole Rowland is a lobbyist, adjunct professor and writer. She enjoys spending her time with family and friends, traveling, reading novels and empowering women whom have left relationships as a result of domestic violence.


## ABOUT THE ILLUSTRATOR

Jamil Burton is a professional artist and illustration painter. Jamil formally trained at Savannah Art & Design at St. Paul's College. He has illustrated several children's books, "Nora's Lollipop", "Oli Learns to Read" and "Hannah's World." Jamil has also completed numerous commissions professionally for various organizations such as The United Way, Mount Vernon High School and Williford Elementary School.